A Lawyer's Guide Through Probate

I0049083

Quick Overview of The Process

Executing a probate can be a complex and legally sensitive process, as it involves settling the affairs of a deceased person and distributing estate assets to beneficiaries or heirs. The specific steps can vary depending on your jurisdiction, so it's essential to consult with an attorney or legal professional experienced in probate law.

1. **Confirm the Death:** Obtain at least six (6) death certificates and more if there are properties owned in multiple counties of Oklahoma. You will need this document for many different parts of the probate process.
2. **Hire an Attorney:** Consider hiring an experienced probate attorney to guide you through the process, as probate laws can be complex.
3. **Identify the Executor or Personal Representative:** If there is a will, it typically designates an executor. If there is no will, the court will appoint a personal representative. The executor or personal representative is responsible for managing the estate.
4. **Gather Documents and Information:**
   - Locate and secure the deceased's will (if one exists), and make sure you know if it is an original or a copy.
   - Collect financial documents, such as bank statements, investment accounts, property deeds, and insurance policies, as well as titles to vehicles.
   - Create an inventory of the deceased's assets and debts. (You can use the pages at the back of this Guide)
5. **File a Petition:** Your attorney will help you prepare and file a petition with the probate court to open the probate estate. This initiates the formal legal probate process.
6. **Notify Heirs and Beneficiaries:** Notify all interested parties, including heirs, beneficiaries, and creditors, of the probate proceedings. This will involve publishing a notice in a local newspaper and mailing copies of the Petition to all known creditors and identified beneficiaries, as well as heirs.
7. **Validate the Will (if applicable):** The court will determine whether the will is an original or be asked to validate a copy. If it is valid, it will guide the distribution of assets. The court will determine asset distribution based on Oklahoma law if there is no will. Again, it helps to have an attorney assist with this process.
8. **Manage Assets:**
   - Open an estate bank account to manage and consolidate the deceased's liquid assets.
   - Maintain, protect, and manage all of the assets during the probate process. If there is a house, it must be secured, locks changed and insurance verified.
9. **Pay Debts and Taxes:**
   - Identify and notify creditors of the estate as required.
   - Do not pay valid priority debts, including funeral expenses and hospital bills, until you determine how much money is available to the estate.
10. **File an Inventory:** Provide an inventory of the estate's assets and their estimated values to the court unless the inventory can be waived.
11. **Claims.** There is a statutory process for handling claims and selling property of the estate, they must be followed to avoid liability.
12. **File an Accounting:** Prepare a detailed Final Account of all estate transactions, including income and expenses, and submit it to the court for approval.
13. **Obtain Court Approval:** Seek court approval for the final distribution of assets and the closing of the estate.
14. **Close the Estate:** After the court approves the final distribution and settles any remaining issues, you can close the estate.

15. **File Final Reports:** File final reports with the court, confirming that all estate matters have been properly settled.
16. **Release of Executor/Personal Representative:** If you are the executor or personal representative, make sure the court formally releases you from your duties.
17. **Final Tax Returns:** File the deceased's final income tax returns and any estate tax returns as required <u>before</u> closing the probate.
18. **Distribution of Inheritance:** Distribute the remaining assets to the beneficiaries according to the court's instructions and Final Order.

Introduction

Welcome to "Your Guide to Filing a Probate Petition With or Without an Attorney". (We respectfully suggest you hire an attorney.) If you are holding this book, it is likely that you are facing a situation where you need to file pleadings in a court of law, and you are hesitant to hire an attorney due to the costs involved. We understand that legal matters can be intimidating, and the thought of navigating the complexities of the probate legal system on your own can be overwhelming. Hopefully this book will help you along the way.

Filing a petition to probate an estate with or without a will, on your own, might seem like a daunting task, but it is possible with the right guidance and information. By the time you finish reading this book, you will have a better understanding of the process, the confidence to take action, and the knowledge to make informed decisions about your case.

If you need help:
Woska Law Firm, PLLC
awoska@woskalawfirm.com
405-657-8251

What You Can Expect from This Book:

Clear, Step-by-Step Guidance: We'll walk you through filing a petition, from understanding the basics to preparing and submitting your documents.

Practical Tips and Strategies: You'll find valuable tips and strategies to maximize your chances of success in court.

Legal Terminology Made Simple: We'll demystify legal jargon and explain complex terms in plain language so you can confidently navigate the legal system.

Common Pitfalls to Avoid: Learn about common mistakes people make when representing themselves and how to avoid them.

Checklists and Templates: We provide useful checklists and templates to help you organize your case and ensure you're not missing any crucial details.

Additional Resources: Throughout the book, you'll find references to online resources, legal aid organizations, and support networks that can further assist you in your journey.

Real-Life Stories: We share stories of individuals who have successfully filed petitions without an attorney, demonstrating that it's entirely possible for you to do the same.

By the time you finish reading this book, you'll be well-equipped to navigate the legal system with confidence. Remember, you have the right to access justice, and you don't have to go it alone. "Your Guide to Filing a Petition Without an Attorney" is your companion on this empowering journey towards resolving your legal matter.

So, let's get started and take the first step toward asserting your rights and achieving a favorable outcome in your case. You've got this!

Helpful Things To Remember:

- You must first determine what cash and assets are in the estate.

- The estate can only pay expenses if it has enough money. The better records you keep, the more accurate your reimbursement will be as the Personal Representative as set out by statute.

- Scan the applicable QR Codes with your phone to go to links to the items.

- Determine how much money is owed to hospitals, doctors, and nursing homes, as well as ambulance companies.

- Social Security: Notify the Social Security Administration of decedent's death, return the benefits received in the month of death, and inquire about survivor's benefits, if applicable.

- Veterans Affairs: If applicable, contact the Department of Veterans Affairs to inquire about death, burial, and survivor benefits.

- Cancellations: Cancel the decedent's subscriptions (newspapers, magazines), utility services (cable television, telephone), personal service contracts (landscaping, house cleaning), and health insurance coverage. Ask for refunds, if possible.

- Safe Deposit Boxes: Access, inventory, and take possession of the contents.

- Valuables: Compile an inventory and take custody of all valuable personal property, such as art, jewelry, and collectibles.

- Insurance Coverage: Contact the decedent's insurance carriers to secure comprehensive insurance coverage for all estate assets during the probate process and/or to ensure property and casualty insurance coverage continues on personal effects, automobiles, real estate, and any goods in storage.

– Insurance Benefits: Investigate insurance benefits including life insurance, accidental death insurance, and possible credit life policies for mortgages, credit cards, and auto loans.

– Employment Benefits: Contact decedent's employer regarding unpaid wages and investigate existence of any employment sponsored death benefits or pensions due.

– Unclaimed Property: Search Oklahoma's unclaimed property database: www.oktreasure.com.

– Credit Cards: Notify credit bureaus of death and cancel and destroy all credit cards, but do not pay credit card bills without first consulting with your probate attorney.

– Business Interests: Arrange for the management of any business and decide if it should be sold.

– Non-Estate Assets: For all assets that automatically pass upon the decedent's death to a beneficiary other than the estate (e.g., life insurance policies, Pay-on-Death accounts, Transfers-on-Death deeds, social security benefits, and retirement accounts), notify the beneficiaries so they can collect the proceeds themselves.

– Annual Accounting: If probate takes longer than one year, prepare an accounting of all receipts and disbursements of the estate to file with the court, unless it has waived this requirement.

– Notify Creditors: Within two months of being appointed executor or administrator, identify and notify all creditors of their opportunity to present claims. Then, receive their claims.

– Asset Distribution: Transfer remaining estate assets to beneficiaries (e.g., write checks for cash distributions, transfer assets in-kind by re-registering ownership or arranging for rollovers, execute real estate deeds, establish and fund any trusts created by the will, etc.) and obtain a written receipt and release from each beneficiary.

Initial Dates to Remember:

Date of Death _____

**Date of Hearing on Petition
to Probate Estate** _____

**Date of Filing Affidavit of
Mailing** _____

**Date of Order Admitting Will
To Probate or Opening Probate
Estate** _____

**Date of Personal Representative
Appointment** _____

Date of Notice to Creditors _____

Date Creditor's Claims are Due _____

1

What To Do Now That You Have Completed Your Petition?

A petition for the probate of a will must show:

1. The jurisdictional facts;
2. Whether the person named as executor consents to act, or renounces his right to the letters testamentary;
3. The names, ages, and residence of the heirs, legatees, and devisees of the decedent, so far as known to the petitioner;
4. The probate value and character of the property of the estate;
5. The name of the person for whom letters testamentary are prayed.

The petition for the probate of a will must be in writing and signed by the applicant or his counsel.

A completed Petition will need to be signed and the original Will filed or the copy of the original attached.

Be sure to read the Petition very carefully and make any necessary corrections before you sign it, as you are stating under oath that the Petition is true and correct to the best of your knowledge. You are also asking the court to find that the Will submitted meets all the statutory requirements for a valid will.

Take the original Petition and at least 2 copies to the county court clerk for filing. The Court Clerk will keep the original and will file-stamp your copies. This is when you will pay the initial court costs, get assigned a case number and a judge (you will use this assigned case number on all future pleadings).

*Remember to add fees to expense ledger

Applicable County Court Clerk

The Petition then needs to be set for hearing. In many counties you will take one copy of the file stamped petition to the assigned judge's clerk and get a date set for a hearing. In a few counties the Court Clerk that takes your original Petition will give you the court date.

You will fill out and present the assigned Judge's Clerk the Order for Hearing and Notice of Hearing with that information and once a date and time is determined, you take them back to the court clerk to file in the case. The court clerk will keep the original of the Order and the Notice for the court file, so be sure to keep at least 2 copies for yourself and one for each of the others on the Affidavit of Mailing which must all be filed after mailing is complete.

Next, mail a copy of the Notice of Hearing, the Order and the Petition to all of the people listed on the affidavit of mailing. You will file the affidavit of mailing after you mail the Notice of Hearing and before the date of the hearing. Use regular first-class mail. Certified mail is not needed. The judge assigned to your case has to make sure you have notified all interested parties by mail.

You will also publish the notice with a newspaper of general circulation in the county and make sure a proof of publication of the Petition is filed. The court clerk can assist you in finding the correct publisher for the Notice. In many counties, there is a drop box in the courthouse where you can leave the Notice to be picked up by the publisher. Please note that there is a fee for the publication and you can usually pay that to the court clerk. If the publisher does not file an affidavit of publication (many do, but some do not) then you will need to call the publisher and obtain and file the affidavit in the court file before the day of your hearing. If you go to the hearing without the proof of publication, the judge may have to reschedule your case until the proof can be shown.

2

What Is Likely To Happen At The First Hearing?

Unless you have an attorney, at the first hearing you will want to arrive a few minutes early and sit in the audience area of the courtroom to wait for your case to be called. When called you will normally be permitted to approach the judge's bench with your proof of publication, your signed and notarized affidavit of mailing, the Letters that authorize you, as personal representative, to act on behalf of the probate estate, and the Order admitting the Will or opening the estate. Provide these to the judge to be signed and returned to you. You will then take these originals, and make at least two copies of each, to the court clerk to be filed and stamped. You should ask the court clerk to Certify at least two copies of the Letters and one copy of the court order which you will then use to transact business for the probate estate.

3

You Just Finished the First Hearing, What Now?

Keep a certified copy of the Order and Letters in your possession when you transact business for the estate. These are the documents that give you authority. You may need to buy extra death certificates from the Oklahoma Department of Vital Statistics in the event you must produce proof of decedent's death to banks or others.

To get a certified copy of a death certificate, you fill out a request form provided by your vital records office.

-Name of the deceased person
-Name of the deceased's parents
-Date of death
-City of death
-Last address of the deceased person
-Your relationship to the deceased person

**Scan to get A
Death Certificate**

Oklahoma Vital Records
Vital Records Division
P.O. Box 248964
Oklahoma City, OK, 73124
Phone 877-817-7364
Fax 866-550-1852

4

Where Should I Look For Creditors? How Do I Know I Have Made A Good Faith Search?

You can look for creditors by picking up the mail of the decedent and watching for bills of every type. It often takes a few months to assure yourself that the known creditors of the decedent are identified. (A good idea is to set up a P.O. Box to receive the decedent's mail because if you forward to your address you will receive decedent's mail for years.)

You should ask those most familiar with the decedent if they know of any creditors with a possible claim against the decedent's estate.

If the decedent passed away in a hospital, the law states that you must include the hospital as a potential creditor, as well as physicians and nursing homes.

Once you have notified all the creditors and their date to file claims has passed, you must determine which claims are approved and which are not approved. This may lead to probate litigation over a claim.

5

What Should I Do About Keeping Records of Income and Expenses?

It would be wise to keep a separate book (it could be a 3-ring notebook or a spiral notebook) of all probate income and expenses and make sure you keep receipts. If the decedent received social security, notify the bank of the death. The bank may have to return the last payment received from Social Security. If the decedent is receiving income from rent or oil and gas interests, you need to keep track of where they are coming from.

If there were retirement checks coming in, determine if they cease as of the date of death.

Keep records of your expenses, including your mileage (include the reason for the trip) and any costs you have paid, like the filing fee, the notice(s) published by the newspaper, as these can be reimbursed to you out of the decedent's money once the Order Approving Final Account of the Probate is entered. The better you are about keeping detailed records along with receipts, the easier it will be to complete the probate.

6

Do I Need To Do An Income Tax Return?

It is always wise to talk to the decedent's accountant or tax preparer. If the decedent did not use one of these, look for a copy of the decedent's tax return for the most recent years (but remember that many people need not file tax returns if their income is low enough). Often there will be a tax return due, and you should be sure it is filed on time. If you are not familiar with how to prepare and file taxes, it would be wise to meet with a bookkeeper or accountant to make sure that the proper tax returns are filed both for the decedent or the decedent's estate if it has enough income during the time that the probate is open. The cost of preparing tax returns is normally an expense of the estate.

7

What Do I Do and Say At The Bank To Get The Money?

When you go to the bank, take a copy of the Order appointing you as the Personal Representative and your Letters and advise the Bank that you are the court authorized personal representative. The bank should then allow you to obtain information concerning all accounts belonging to the decedent and accumulate the information on how much money is available for the payment of creditors and beneficiaries. If the bank account does not have a joint tenant or a beneficiary, the bank should turn the money over to you as the Personal Representative. This money should be deposited into the estate bank account.

8

How Do I Open A Checking Account For The Probate?

You will take your letters testamentary and the order admitting the will to probate to the bank. You will meet with one of the agents for the bank and open a bank account for the probate estate. You will first need to get a tax ID number for the estate (see next topic). There should not be a problem opening an account for the probate as long as you have money to deposit in the account. When you set the account up, all of the paperwork for the account should come to you as the personal representative, not you individually, but it can be mailed to your address.

9

How Do I Get A Tax ID Number For The Probate?

You can scan the code below or go online and go to www.IRS.Gov. This will take you to IRS sites and forms. The form you need to fill out is the form for obtaining an employer identification number for a probate estate. At the top right of the IRS website you will find a block that allows you to conduct a search. Search for "EIN Online". You will be taken to a short questionnaire you fill out and you can receive the tax identification number immediately. Please remember to save that number very carefully and provide it to the CPA or bookkeeper preparing tax returns.

EIN
Application

10

I Am Pretty Sure Medicare Paid All Of The Medical Bills. Why Do I Need To Send a Notice To Creditors To The Hospital?

If you do not notify third parties of the probate and the deadline to make claims against the estate for unpaid bills, this will become a problem in the future, as that must be done before a Final Account distribution can be completed by the court. It is always a best course of action to send a Notice to Creditors to anyone who may claim that they are owed money by the decedent. At the time of the Final Account hearing, you will notify the court by an appropriate pleading you file that you have notified every known creditor and the only ones that filed claims were the ones you identify and agree to pay, and then a Final Order can be entered, cutting off the rights of all of the other creditors that you notified.

If the deceased person passed away in a hospital, you must always send a Notice to Creditors to the hospital. The Oklahoma Supreme Court has ruled that the hospital where one dies is always presumed to be a potential creditor so they must be given the Notice to Creditors. You must also put the hospital on the affidavit of mailing so that the judge will know that you have completed this task.

11

Where Do I Find Legal Descriptions Of The Land That Belongs To The Probate?

You will need to get the legal description of any real property that the decedent owned in his or her name. One way to find the needed description is to get a copy of any deeds that were held in the name of the decedent. Sometimes a decedent will have a file cabinet or a box or place that they keep important papers. If you can find the box, you may find a copy of the deed. If the decedent owned rental properties or minerals, you are going to need the legal descriptions for those as well. You are also able to go to the county clerk where the decedent owned property at the time of death and ask the county clerk if they can search by the decedent's name to determine if the decedent owned any property or owed any debts that are registered with the county clerk's office. If they find anything, they can provide you with a copy of the document for a small fee.

12

How To Fill Out These Forms?

When you fill out forms relating to the probate of the decedent's estate, you must provide the required information. The information that is requested in forms is often required by law according to statutes relating to probates in the State of Oklahoma. Never use a social security number belonging to the decedent in any forms you fill out. You can only use the last 4 digits of the social security number.

(Example, ***-**-4444)

13

Why Does The
Court Need This Information?

A probate is a transfer of title from the decedent to his or beneficiaries. As a result, the court is required to administer and facilitate the transfer of title for personal property and real property so that the legal title is transferred from the decedent to the people that the decedent wanted to receive their property upon death. That is why the information is requested by the court.

14

How Do I Determine What Creditors Exist?

It is very important to identify a creditor, a creditor's address and the account number, and the amount of money that is supposedly owed to that creditor. You should start by gathering all the mail that comes to the decedent. Watch the mail for bills, evidence of credit cards, and any other information that might lead to a creditor or to insurance. You should also go online to determine whether the deceased person has been sued, as this is strong evidence of a debt that you may need to address. Be sure to consider potential medical bills. Did the ambulance respond to a call? Was there an emergency room visit? Was there a contract for a cell phone, a security system, a mortgage, utility bills, back taxes?

15

How To Prepare An Inventory?

The simplest way to prepare an inventory is to divide it into personal property and real property. The real property would include the title to a house, oil and gas interest, or mineral interest, and personal property would include furniture, fixtures, equipment, tools, guns, ammunition, paintings, rugs, or other things that would be in the house or in storage for the decedent. You will need to prepare an inventory because you are required to tell the court what the approximate value of all real and personal property is, and it is sometimes easier to come up with those values by breaking things into parts, like tools would have a value based on what somebody is willing to pay for all the tools.

You may be selling all real and personal property during the probate. This requires the use of Motions and notices according to statute and is made easier if you hire an attorney to help you with the probate.

16

How To Locate Title To Property And Automobiles?

The title to property (houses and land) can be located by going to the county clerk and asking them to run a title check to see if any real property is held in the decedent's name. With respect to automobiles, you are going to have to find the title to the auto. If you cannot find the title, you are going to have to get the VIN of the automobile from the front of the car, you have to look through the windshield to find it, and you can send in for a lost tag or a lost title. Again, you have to go online, find the form, fill it out and send it in, or take it in to a tag agency.

17

What Do You Do With Social Security Payments After Death?

The easiest way to deal with Social Security is to take the proof of death to the deceased person's bank or to the Social Security office nearest you. The bank will notify Social Security electronically, and then will return to Social Security any check that the estate is not allowed to keep.

18

How To Determine The Cost Of The Last Illness?

Fortunately, the creditors who claim that they have a priority in getting paid because they provided care for the final illness have to support that claim with proof in the form of invoices or statements. If there is a dispute as to which creditors will or will not get paid, you are likely going to have to talk with an attorney.

Creditor's claims are a significant matter with the numerous statutes involved. Handling creditor's claims is best done with the help of a probate attorney familiar with the statutes.

19

How To Publish A Notice In The Newspaper?

Every county has a publisher who is authorized to publish Notices in probate cases, and all of the court clerks can assist you in identifying the correct publisher. The number of publications required and the amount of time permitted to respond are all statutory. Do not try to handle publications without understanding the statutes or having an attorney help you. Some court clerks have drop boxes in their offices where the publisher picks up the legal notices to be published. In other counties you must deliver the Notice to the publisher's office. No matter how the Notice gets to the publisher, be sure to find out how to pay and where to pay as otherwise the publisher will not provide proof of publication which is required by the court.

Keeping Track of Your Information

Things to track:

1. All your expenses
2. Inventory of all Assets
3. Bills from all Creditors
4. All checking, savings or brokerage accounts
5. All vehicles
6. All deeds
7. Make an Application for "Unclaimed Property" with the State.
8. All Creditor's Claims
9. All monies in and out

Estate of _____

Checklist	Expense Cost	Date of Completion	✔
Initial Court			☐
Petition			☐
Will			☐
Extra Death Certificate			☐
Tax Preparation			☐
			☐
			☐
			☐
			☐
			☐
			☐
			☐
			☐
			☐

Case Number _____

Estate of _____

Expenses Owed	Account Number	Expense Cost	Date Paid	✔
				☐
				☐
				☐
				☐
				☐
				☐
				☐
				☐
				☐
				☐
				☐
				☐
				☐

Estate of _____

Inventory   **Value**

_____

_____

_____

_____

_____

_____

_____

_____

_____

_____

_____

_____

_____

_____

_____

_____

_____

_____

_____

Estate of _____

Inventory   **Value**

_____

_____

_____

_____

_____

_____

_____

_____

_____

_____

_____

_____

_____

_____

_____

_____

_____

Case Number _____

Estate of _____

Inventory   **Value**

_____

_____

_____

_____

_____

_____

_____

_____

_____

_____

_____

_____

_____

_____

_____

_____

_____

_____

Case Number _____

Estate of _____

Inventory   **Value**

_____

_____

_____

_____

_____

_____

_____

_____

_____

_____

_____

_____

_____

_____

_____

_____

www.ingramcontent.com/pod-product-compliance
Lightning Source LLC
Chambersburg PA
CBHW051802200326
41597CB00025B/4655